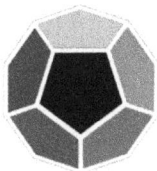

ENTER THE FLOW

THE

FLOW

The Elite Goaltender's Guide to Performance

OPERATION DODECAHEDRON

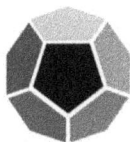

ENTER THE FLOW

The Elite Goaltender's Guide to Performance

For more information, please visit

operationdodecahedron.com

Operation Dodecahedron ISBN: 979-8-9914516-1-1

"There is no position in sport
as noble as goaltending."

-Vladislav Tretiak

INTRODUCTION

No doubt you are aware that playing hockey goalie is a difficult task. See, right there is where you're wrong. You don't play goalie. You are a goalie. Or maybe you're not. Either way, you're about to find out. It's good that you picked up this book, you have a lot to learn.

There exists a force so powerful we cannot speak its true name. The Taoist calls it *wu wei*. A scientist might term it sub-neural effluence. Our ancient ancestors surely thought of it as magic, the breath of the gods flowing around and through them. It exists as a state somewhere between thought and action, reach and grasp. Letting go of forced effort. Perfect harmony with the universe itself. When the rhythms of life sync up and drop with perfect alignment into some narrow groove in our human brain and for a few brief moments, we transcend ourselves. It is beyond the scope of this book and the powers of its writer to name this phenomenon, but for our purposes, we will call it Flow.

Flow is elusive, darting from the mind at thought's shadow, yet a goaltender can learn to cultivate it with ritual, mindset, and intention. This book, *Enter the Flow: The Elite Goaltender's Guide to Performance*, is a map to the mastery of presence, discipline, and clarity. It is about understanding that elite goaltending is not a destination, but a path connecting mind, body, and puck in ways that defy explanation with clunky words. To enter the Flow is to find stillness within chaos, to embrace solitude as a source of strength, and to lead not by words, but by unwavering confidence and performance in the crease.

Hockey goaltending is a way of life and like life, it is a fucking paradox: you're part of a team, but alone. It's a mental test within a physical game. The job is to save them all, but some will get past you.

Becoming an elite goalie is a test of will, a pursuit that rewards absolute presence and punishes even the smallest lapse of focus. Elite goalies do not merely react. They enter a state of being where the game slows, they move with effortless power and decisive precision and the puck will draw to their body. This is not ability, not explanation. This is not talent. This is not skill. This is not luck. This is Flow.

Hockey is a game of speed, aggression, and unpredictability. The goaltender, however, must be the eye of the storm. The moment you allow distractions, fear, or swirling doubt to cloud your mind, the game will consume you. The goal of this book is to teach you how to master your mental environment, stop being a pussy, and cultivate the habits and rituals that will allow you to shed thought and simply *be* in the moment. The elite goalie does not think about making a save; he simply *makes* the save. This is the mind-body-puck connection, a harmony that can only be achieved through discipline, self-awareness, and a willingness to completely surrender the future as a sacrifice to the present.

There are sixteen sections in the book. Read them in any order and return to them as needed. At the end of every section, there will be several pathways to Flow that have worked for numerous elite goalies. There is a season's worth of journal pages in the back.

In the following pages, you will explore the principles that lead to peak performance. You will learn to build pre-game rituals that set the stage for peak focus, how to train your mind to silence distractions, and how to cultivate the habits that will allow you to perform under pressure. You will examine leadership, energy, confidence, the rewards of working in solitude, the power of visualization and the beauty of the small moments that define a goaltender's life.

The road to becoming an elite goaltender is not one of brute force or natural talent alone. It is a path of patience, presence, and relentless self-mastery. It is about learning to embrace pressure, to welcome hardship, and to trust the instincts that you have sharpened through hours of grinding dedication. It is about finding joy between whistles, about seeking beauty. Above all, it is about learning to let go, to exist fully in the now.

I agreed to write this book only if my name wouldn't be on it. Not because I lack conviction in the ideals, but because paths to Flow are no one man's story to tell. You can call me Goalie 1 and I was a fucking elite goalie.

PREPARATION

Time bends differently in the hours before you stand in the crease. The puck exists in all possible trajectories simultaneously and to be there, to be *everywhere*, you need to dissolve the membrane between preparation and performance until they're just one continuous breath.

The day before a game, engage in conversation with it. Thinking about it, wondering about it, worrying about it, that's the trap. Welcome the game as an old friend who knows all your secrets.

The morning of a game, practice gratitude, seek humility, beseech karma.

At the rink, the portal opens. Three hours before the puck drops, the building is whispering instead of shouting. Touch the metal doorframe entering the dressing room.

The gear is fun, obviously. Piece by piece, same order every time. Construct the self that can enter Flow. Each strap pulled is another layer of protection from the puck and an ordinary existence. Where others see details, you see patterns.

During the anthem, balance on your blades between readiness and relaxation. Focus on nothing, see everything. Breathe deeply. Feel your heartbeat slow as the building's pulse quickens.

The puck drops and you're there, waiting.

If you're reading this, you're already prepared.

Pathways to Flow:

Greatness is not accidental.
Willingness comes before.

Asceticism is Greek for training.

This information cannot be
learned in any school.

The results will seem like déjà vu.

Note what hand the opponents are.
Strengths and weaknesses.

Goalie Mastery.

MIND

Marcus Aurelius would've been an elite goalie. He said, "You have power over your mind—not outside events. Realize this, and you will find strength."

You stand in the crease. The crowd screams. This is not your concern. The score is zero-zero or five-to-one but both are equally unreal, constructs of measurement that exist outside the eternal now and you believe that this matters. It does not matter. You believe the game depends on you. It does not depend on you. The puck will go where the puck goes, following laws as old as ice itself. Your task is to stop what can be stopped.

Thoughts, distractions, regrets, fears, pain and hockey pucks. They're coming right at you. Greet them with your hands.

Empty the mind, and the body becomes water. Water does not decide to flow, it simply flows. The butterfly does not require thought when thought has been eliminated.

The goalie who thinks, "I am tracking the puck" has already lost. The elite goalie is one with the puck.

Pathways to Flow:

Mental reps are (almost)
as good as physical.

Be in the n.o.w. Narrow. Offense. Win.

Rhythm of mind and body produce Flow.

Engage your body, but disengage
your mind at every opportunity.

If you apply what you learn in these pages,
you will become superhuman.

The elite goalie's mind is the world's
most powerful computer.

Your mind doesn't know what
exists and what it creates.

BODY

Your body is a fortress, the first line of defense against 100 mph clappers that would kill a lesser man.

Flexibility isn't just about sucking your own dick, it's the difference between a desperation paddle save and watching the lamp light up while you're sprawled like frozen roadkill.

Stretch hips twice daily, three times a day in summer. The stretch is about listening to what the body knows that the mind hasn't learned yet. Pour looseness into yourself.

Size helps, no two ways about it. No amount of Flow is going to help a 5'4" goalie cover the corners. Have you thought about soccer or gymnastics?

The elite goalie has elite reflexes. Reaction time separates the saved from the damned. Train your thoughts, words and actions to fire without hesitation until your hands move like cobra strikes.

Your body knows things before your mind does.

Trust the vessel. Touch the limit.

The puck doesn't care about your excuses.

Avoid racquet sports.

Beer is fine.

Pathways to Flow:

Keep your hips and hands loose.

Mind provides belief, body provides strength.
You must have one to create the other.

Do the exercise. Now. Right now.

See the puck spinning from stick
all the way to your body.

Drop into your butterfly as you visualize.

Drill: Overlap to RVH entries.

SPIRIT

Spirit is hope doubled. It's very contagious and it can be snuffed out like a candle if you take your eye off the puck for one damn second.

The elite goaltender's spirit isn't some paper you pin to a corkboard in the dressing room. It's the thing that keeps him standing when thirty thousand people are screaming for his blood.

Why do you think they call booze spirits? Discipline is the bottle, but spirit is the truth at the bottom.

Your team doesn't follow "strategy." They follow *belief*. When everything's burning, on the edge of collapse, they will look to you, the masked oracle between the pipes. They must see your spirit.

The goalie's spirit opens that portal by surrendering control while maintaining total focus. It's a contradiction. It's beautiful. It's the moment the universe forgets you exist and you become pure instinct.

And when do you reach Flow? Brother, Flow isn't a destination, it's what happens when you stop thinking and start *being*.

The spirit isn't armor. It's what makes a man worthy of wearing it.

Pathways to Flow:

Flow: Harmony of the five senses and four dimensions.

Seek/create moments of connection with your teammates.

Focus on the puck.

PRESSURE

The thing about pressure in hockey is that it's the rocket fuel that'll either launch a kid into the NHL or leave him twitching behind some suburban rink at 2 AM, wondering why he can't remember what fun feels like.

As the final defender, there is pressure. Holding a one-goal lead with eight minutes left, there is pressure. Killing penalties while your team gasps for oxygen? Pressure. Facing a good team? Pressure. Facing a bad team? More pressure.

Every scenario is pressure wearing a different mask.

The alchemy is this: pressure becomes power the moment you stop treating it like a disease. It's information. It's energy looking for direction. Those good teams? They sharpen your focus to a laser point. That one-goal lead? It turns every save into a statement. The penalty kill? That's your chance to be a fucking superhero while everyone watches.

Where's the line between nonchalance and Flow state? It's closer than you think. Nonchalance pretends nothing matters. Flow knows nothing matters.

Is it necessary to take a shit before the game? If your pregame ritual involves ass-bombing the bathroom so you can face thirty shots unburdened, then yes. Whatever is necessary.

Pressure is the cover charge to get in. Power is what you drink once you're inside.

Once upon a time, there were two goalies facing each other in the finals of a big tournament. Both of them were really feeling the pressure. One guy won and the other guy lost. The end.

Pathways to Flow:

Look good, feel good, play good.

The flow of air binds mind and body.

Remember: Vison and Action. V.A. Victory Always.

This is how you become a legend.

PRESENCE

Presence is not your "aura" and it's not your "vibe." Both important, no doubt, but not as crucial as the ability to maintain focus within the present moment. Flow exists in a delicate balance on a bubble of time.

You got five-holed by a dribbler? That puck's already in the net. Let it haunt you and the next shot's going bar-down while you're still apologizing to ghosts. Presence means hitting reset before the lamp stops spinning.

Worrying about the third period when you're in the first? That's how you let in four goals in six minutes and spend the bus ride home wondering why that girl won't text you back.

The present moment is a ruthless, hard, gorgeous sliver. Thin as a blade edge, sharp enough to cut through every should've and what-if. You have to be quick to catch it, but that's the game. That's the contract you signed when you strapped on the pads.

Every shot is its own story. The one before it is mythology. The one after it is science fiction. Right now: this shooter, this read, this release point is the only thing that's real.

Let's face it. Sometimes you take one in the chest and to make the save, all you had to do was be there.

Pathways to Flow:

Be naked. Self-consciousness hinders performance.

There's no name for it, for as soon as you think, it disappears.

Action is the force multiplier.

SOLITUDE

The goalie is alone even when surrounded. Part of the team but fundamentally separate, the goalie is a different species skating the same ice. While your teammates hunt in packs, you stand vigil in your crease like some feral monk who traded companionship for stoic vision.

They won't understand your rituals. They'll call it superstition. Cultivate this mystique. Let them wonder what you're thinking back there, why you're so calm when everything's breaking down. Your secrets are currency.

The secrets are spoken in grunt and scream in the dark so that you shine in the brightest light. The extra lifts, the film study at midnight, the thousand butterfly pushes nobody's counting. That's how legends get assembled, piece by lonely piece.

The paradox is this: you're the most isolated player on the team and the most essential. Nobody cheers the man who stands alone during those grinding off-season hours when doubt is his only company. But come game time, when he robs their best shooter blind, snatches victory as his due, they fucking cheer then.

And you can hear them nonetheless, even though you're still alone back there, even though you always will be. That's the price. That's the power.

The elite goalie is the last terrible answer to every question the other team asks.

The crease is a kingdom built for one.

Pathways to Flow:

The past is a closed book,
the future a blank page.

If your mind image is clear, you will act without thinking or hesitation when the time comes.

You must act without thinking, react without reason. There is no reason.

Meditation creates power through the absence of thought.

LEADERSHIP

You are first to enter the breach, the first to touch blade to ice.

The elite goalie does not rely upon words alone. In the room, speak sparingly but with purpose. Embody calm certainty. The greatest leaders do not lecture, they challenge, then show their backs.

On the ice, leadership flows through action. Every save declares to your teammates: *I will not break*. Order the chaos. The goalie sees all; thus the goalie must guide all. Communicate to your D-men. Direct the breakout. Your voice cuts through the noise of battle because you alone possess complete vision.

Your teammates will follow you if you embrace burden. While others rotate and rest, you remain. The game is your dominion. In a 60-minute war, you fight every second. Leadership is constancy and constancy is power.

Respect and fear. Your teammates must respect your preparation, your composure under siege, your willingness to accept responsibility for any failure. Your opponents must fear your focus, sensing that nothing will pass. A goalie who radiates unshakable confidence becomes a fortress. The enemy begins to doubt before they shoot.

The crease is your command post. Lead from there, and your team becomes an extension of your will.

Pathways to Flow:

Always be in the now.

Always Be Confident.

Question yourself. Answer.

The persuasion you carry is an advantage.

Mind Map the destination.

An elite goalie is an
elite wingman.

ENERGY

Energy begins before the arena. The elite goaltender understands that physical stamina emerges from disciplined preparation. Two to three hours before battle, consume complex carbohydrates and lean protein: oatmeal with fruit, chicken with rice, pasta with vegetables. Hydrate relentlessly.

Physical energy alone cannot sustain sixty minutes of elite-level hockey. Mental energy requires a different cultivation. It grows out of visualization, through 4-7-8 breathing to prime the mind, through pre-game routines that build psychological armor. Spiritual energy comes from purpose. Why do you guard this net?

Energy dies. It's the law. Entropy is doubt, scattered focus, the weight of past failures carried into present moments. It advances when you stop moving between whistles, when your self-talk turns toxic, when you allow one goal to poison the next period. Fight it by resetting constantly. Slap the posts. Adjust your mask. Drink more water.

The crowd feeds you if you feed them first. Knock someone out of your crease. When you make a good save, acknowledge it with a subtle gesture and watch ten thousand people rise. But cross into arrogance and you become an insufferable dick. The line? Confidence celebrates competence; swagger celebrates self. You know the difference.

And yes, the hair matters. Flow generates mystique, an aesthetic energy that opponents cannot ignore.

Energy is circular: you create it through preparation, sustain it through discipline, share it with your crowd, and receive it back amplified. The elite goalie becomes both generator and conductor, transforming individual voltage into collective electricity.

Pathways to Flow:

Butterfly recovery, power slides, rotations, half-butterfly saves.

Break the game into five minute stages.

Stand confidently and repeat your mantra six times or as time permits.

There's no name for it, for as soon as you even think it, it disappears.

SELF-BELIEF

Self-belief cannot be bought. It is earned when others sleep, through discipline, through pain, through doubt. Each repetition deposits currency into an invisible account, until, when the puck drops, you cash out what you've invested.

Self-belief is not a performance. The elite goaltender has belief in himself even when, *especially when*, no one is watching. The test comes when you stand alone. In solitude, self-belief becomes prayer to the goddess Confidence. Have faith in the hours you've invested, the technique you've refined, the person you've become in the dark church of your empty mind.

When you are the only believer, belief must burn its brightest. Others will eventually see what you've known all along, not because you convinced them with words, but because you proved it, save by save, through the quiet power of unshakeable belief forged in countless invisible hours.

Move with deliberate calm off the ice and righteous fury in the crease. Opponents see it, women see it. They feel the weight of facing someone who believes absolutely. This isn't arrogance. It's the natural expression of preparation meeting purpose.

Can you be over-confident? Of course. When confidence detaches from reality, when you believe effort is no longer necessary, when swagger replaces work. Nothing replaces work.

Pathways to Flow:

When facing the rush, speak a single word mantra to narrow focus.

Confidence is contagious.

What you have learned is the ability to be totally confident and at ease at any time

Avoid gripping the stick too tight.

Create confidence before even feeling the puck.

Without confidence, life is a tough grind.

BALANCE

The elite goalie exists in perpetual equilibrium, weight centered, edges sharp, ready. Physical balance separates those who react from those who anticipate. On the ice, balance means controlling your center of gravity through transitions: butterfly to post, post to stand, stand to butterfly. The goalie who remains balanced recovers faster, moves cleaner, wastes no energy on corrections.

Develop this through deliberate drills. Balance board work trains proprioception and core stability. Use resistance bands to create opposition during lateral movements, forcing your body to find equilibrium under stress. Even simple exercises like catching a medicine ball while standing on one skate rewire your nervous system toward constant adjustment.

But balance extends beyond biomechanics. The goalie who cannot balance success and failure will not survive. A shutout cannot define you, nor can a five-goal collapse. Both are temporary states. Attachment to either creates imbalance, tips you toward arrogance or despair. The elite goalie holds victory and defeat as equal teachers, extracting lessons from both without dwelling in either.

Recognize the signs of imbalance early: when wins make you complacent, when losses make you frantic, when you're changing technique constantly or refusing to adjust at all. Both extremes signal disaster approaching. The remedy? Center yourself. Return to fundamentals. Film review. Honest assessment.

The goalie who masters balance stands unmoved while chaos tilts around him.

Pathways to Flow:

Feel the puck.

Pads must be perfectly sealed to the ice.

You are in the Flow, the Flow is in you.

Impact.

Focus on stance. Balance.
Be in the moment.

DEDICATION

The crowd sees only the glorious save, the outstretched pad, the moment of triumph frozen in celebration. They do not see the mornings you rose in darkness to stretch your hamstrings. They do not count the repetitions of the same lateral push, the same angle work, performed in empty rooms alone with your own labored breath.

The truth the masses cannot comprehend is simply this: greatness is constructed from the accumulation of unremarkable days. Today you will stretch. Tomorrow you will stretch again. And the day after, and the day after that, until the number becomes meaningless and the action becomes as automatic as taking a morning piss. One thousand days of stretching. Two thousand days. What monument does this build? Only the palace of excellence, the temple everyone photographs, but few have entered.

There are no days off because regression never rests. Entropy works ceaselessly. Miss one day and you notice. Miss two and your coach notices. Miss three and your opponent notices, and he will exploit the microscopic degradation you permitted through comfort-seeking.

Find patterns in the details and satisfaction in what others call tedious. The stick-handling drill performed for the ten-thousandth time. The post integration work. The video study of your own mediocre efforts and failings, watched without flinching. These are not punishments but privileges, the price of admission to an elite club.

The elite goaltender understands there are no shortcuts, only the long road walked daily. Show up. Do the work. Repeat. Monotony is your rebellion against limitation, your daily declaration that you will not accept the limits others have accepted. In the grinding, in the showing up, in the tedious miracle of dedication.

Pathways to Flow:

Yes, it's possible.

Elite goalies journal.

Fun fact: it takes 66 reps to make a habit.

The reps build power. Power is everything.

There is no detail too small.

FAILURE

Failure is the dark companion. It arrives uninvited. It knows your weaknesses intimately because it has studied you your whole life. You may bolt the door, you may pray against its coming, but failure possesses the master key.

There are those who say failure should be accepted, like the old wayward friend who drinks all your beer and tries to fuck your girlfriend when you're on the road in Winnipeg. Should you embrace failure? No. Never. But neither should you fear it. Fear breeds paralysis. Hatred breeds recklessness. Instead, regard failure as a severe instructor.

And yet another paradox: failure is your sworn enemy and truest teacher. Success whispers pleasant lies: *You have arrived. You need not improve. Rest now.* But failure screams truth directly into your soul. It shows you the gap between who you are and who you must become. Five goals against? Failure strips away your delusions and presents you with the work that remains.

The elite goalie will sometimes fail to win, but he does not fail. Suffering purifies if you permit it. Each loss becomes a crucible. Will you emerge hardened or broken? The choice reveals character. Those who cannot metabolize failure, who cannot extract its bitter wisdom and grow stronger, these goalies disappear into obscurity. You will use failure's lessons to shine under the brightest light.

Pathways to Flow:

Expect success, don't hope for it.

Fatigue, irritability, pain, shakiness, panic, sweating, light-headedness.

When you get scored on, you are the most powerful man in the rink.

Write down/diagram your successes and failures.

Don't worry about the quality of your writing or drawing.

Overcome fear of the puck (even headshots).

VISUALIZATION

Long before you touch the ice, you must first touch the dream. Close your eyes. Feel the weight of your pads against your legs, the familiar pressure of your blocker, the cool kiss of the mask settling onto your face.

Begin in stillness. Breathe. The rink materializes around you: the white expanse, the blue and the red. The net behind you that you will defend as if it was your own wounded heart. Hear the roar, feel the cold air in your lungs.

The forward's at the left dot. His blue sweater is #77. His stick blade is wrapped with black tape, but the slick puck dances, alive. 77 telegraphs a low shot through shoulder rotation. You power slide left into a half-butter, to meet the puck, pad perfectly sealed to the ice. You hear yourself scream, "Fuck you, 77!," the ref's whistle, the exhalation of your opponent's frustration. Smell the popcorn. All this happens at once and the puck's in your hand.

Do not visualize vaguely. Precision matters. Ninety seconds? Ten minutes? Twenty? An hour? The duration matters less than the fidelity of your vision.

What you rehearse in this timeless realm your body cannot distinguish from actual experience. You are in the only place where your will truly reigns absolute.

Pathways to Flow:

Anticipation will slow the game and allow better play reading.

Visualize shots coming off sticks.

There will be moments you feel have happened before, but only in your mind.

Believe it and you will be be living it. It costs E.

Visualize making 50 saves. Glove, blocker, stick.

Visualize the game in reverse.

Focus on doing visualizations at your absolute best

Your brain is older than words. It works in images.

FLOW IS A CIRCLE

By now, you should have felt it. The odd heat, the feeling of being poised above the bubble.

It's balance. A centering, pathways infinite in every direction. Are you still reading? Do your stretching.

Pathways to Flow:

Be coachable and willing to learn.

The master must become the student.

No man can change the past.
Focus on the present.

The puck is made of vulcanized rubber.
What the fuck are you made of?

The Elite Goaltender keeps a journal.

ABOUT THE AUTHOR

Goalie 1 was an elite goalie. He lives a few miles from the Canadian border.

This is his first book.